1 MONTH OF
FREE
READING

at
www.ForgottenBooks.com

By purchasing this book you are eligible for one month membership to ForgottenBooks.com, giving you unlimited access to our entire collection of over 1,000,000 titles via our web site and mobile apps.

To claim your free month visit:
www.forgottenbooks.com/free180650

ISBN 978-0-483-82930-5
PIBN 10180650

Leisure Hours

—

A BOOK OF SHORT POEMS
ON NATURE

BY

Mrs. Udolphia Davis.

—

PUBLISHED BY THE AUTHOR.

1903
Hornellsville, N. Y.

COPYRIGHT 1903 BY THE AUTHOR.

DEDICATION

INTRODUCTION

This little book, I now before you bring,
And hope within its pages you may find
Some little good, besides amusement, too,
And that the lessons bright may come to you
Without the hard experience that I have seen,
For many trials in my life have been—
But God is kind, and in His love we trust forever-
    more.

THE AUTHOR.

INDEX

Sabbath Morning Meditations

Sweetly solemn is the hour,
'Tis the holy Sabbath morning ;
Bells are chiming and their power,
Sheddeth o'er our hearts a warning,
Which the sunshine can't dispel ;
For we feel that we are mortal,
But the shadows, it will quell,
Which will come unto the portal
Of our hearts in shape of fears,
Knocking for admission there.
But the sunshine of God's love
Will not let our hearts despair.
Solitude w   .o us good,
If it shedd .h o'er our spirits
The sweet balm of Jesus' love,
And thro' faith we do accept it ;
For He watcheth with great care
O'er us here where He has placed us
In His immortality,
All sufficient to protect us.
And in vain He maketh none,
This great Author of our being—
When our mission here is done,
Shall we then in Spirits seeing

Other missions farther on?
In God's care and love advancing
Nearer still the Living Son,
Ever still our lives be living.
We may not know the mysteries of the grave,
But we can trust His all-sufficient love
To guide us o'er the deep, dark, misty wave,
And land us safely in our Home above.

Sunset

Small, fleecy clouds lay all so fair,
Around the sun's bright, dashing glare,
Which in its golden beauty lay
Just above the hills away.

And a merry sound heard I,
Of a little rivulet, passing by,
It made sweet music in my ear,
As it did all my senses cheer.

The hens and chickens—they did steal
Around, to pick their evening meal,
By the door where I was sitting,
As I sat there so busy writing.

And the trees stood out with their leaves of red,
And yellow and green in many a shade ;
For it was now in late September,
As I do so well remember.

The golden corn lay ready for the gleaning,
The grain and grass had all been laid in store,
And the sun sent its bright rays earthward
    streaming,
As it did in days of yore.

(11)

The little birds their homeward way were wend-
    ing,
Then the sun went down and all was shaded o'er,
And for awhile I sat there, busy thinking,
I then arose, came in, and shut the door.

But the beauty of the sunset I had witnessed,
Lay arouud me like a halo in the gloom,
Helping to dispel each thought of sadness,
Leaving only peace and joy within the room.

Nature's Teachings

Wave, sweet meadow, wet with dew,
   Like some lovely lake of silver,
Waving, rocking, to and fro,
   Shining in thy morning splendor.

From whence came thy armor bright?
   Was it scattered down from Heaven?
Holy tears from eyes of light,
   Angels unto Earth hath given?

And within thy shelt'ring fold,
   The buttercups, their heads are peeping,
Glistening there like drops of gold,
   Company for the daisies keeping.

But one other form doth lurk,
   As within our lives, the end,
Looming up its head so dark,
   Comes the ugly prickly thistle.

Just so annoyances will come,
   To our lives, however pleasant,
Like the shadows, o'er the sun,
   And the thistle in the meadow.

But the dew God sendeth down,

On just and unjust, both together,
Not upon the flowers alone,
But upon the thistles ever.

Let us then a lesson learn,
That will bring to us a pleasure,
Let our kind deeds fall upon,
Enemy and friend together.

The Railroad Man

It was past the midnight hour, the moon shone bright,
A railroad man went forth from cottage white,
His fond good-bye he'd said to wife so dear,
His little boy he'd kissed—no tho't of fear.

His lantern in his hand, and down the street
The frosty boards beneath his tread did creak,
As he ran on so swiftly to the train—
No thought that he would ne'er go forth again.

Unto the track he went, the train came on,
And in the frog, he caught his boot so strong.
His boot came off, but there the poor man lay,
Beneath the bloody wheels, all mangled lay.

No one could tell just how the deed was done,
His foot was caught—the thundering train came on,
There was no blame—the brothers gathered round,

Did what they could ; of him they all were fond.

"I am so weary, kind friends," he said,
"Please take me home and lay me on my bed."
With surgeons, brothers, students, in a crowd,
And him on a litter, all came down the road.

Back to the cottage, they with sadness bore
Him through the gate, and knocking at the door—
The wife and child so soundly slept within,
She heard the knocking as but in a dream.

And still the knocking came with louder stroke,
And with a startled cry, she then awoke,
She asked them then, what could the matter be,
With trembling limbs she hastened there to see.

"There has been an accident," a voice replied,
"We have your husband lying here, outside,"
"Do not be frightened, we hope for the best,"
Then the door was opened and in they pressed.
"Do not be worried, dear, for all is well ;"
And unto her the worst they did not tell.

Just as the morning bells were pealing,
And the morning sun came stealing
In the room where he was lying,
All so still, Death's angel came.

When the funeral rites were said,
On the hillside he was laid,
Poor wife's heart would sure be broken—
Had he not left her this token—
"All is well."

The Storm

Oh hark, I hear so gently dropping,
On the window slowly dropping—
The sound of rain so sweetly falling—
   Falling on my ear.

Through the window there comes gleaming,
A light so fierce 'tis fairly startling ;
But what is there to be fearing ?
   I am not afraid.

Then a crash of thunder, pealing—
Awful—grand—sublime—'tis stealing
Through my senses ; and rain is falling
   Faster, faster, still.

Falling—dashing—slashing—clashing—
Rain and thunder loudly crashing ,
'Tis the Voice of God—He's speaking—
   Speaking unto me.

" Oh Lord," I say, " What art Thou wanting?
Here Thy servant sitteth, waiting,
And I hear Thy wondrous speaking—
   I am heeding, Lord."

Then the sun comes brightly gleaming,
And my humble room is filling
With its glory, God is smiling—
   Wondrous, wondrous, smile.

And in Heaven, His bow He setteth,

So that I may not forgetteth,
Who has spoken, in the thunder,
 To His humble child.

Lord, I thank Thee for this token,
Thou unto my soul hast given,
Watch and guard me, Lord, with care,
 Keep, oh keep, Thy child.

Spring.

O bright, sweet time of smiles and tears,
 With hopes of better days to come,
Regrets and trouble, fears and trials,
 We leave behind with winter's storms.

Soft winds and sun have melted soon,
 The snow that lay upon the ground ;
Children come trooping in the room,
 And leave their muddy foot-prints 'round.

Beautiful Spring, thy smile doth bring
 Joy and gladness into our hearts,
And we would fling unto the wind,
 All of our troubles and bid them depart.

The little bird's song, all the day long,
 Fills us with joy, wild wonder and gladness,
And we would wrong this beautiful morn,
 Were we to harbor in our hearts sadness.

Oh that thy smile might for awhile,
    Linger with us in this world of woe,
But unto us all, there surely must fall,
    Sometime through life, care and sorrow, we
        know.

But if our share seems hard to bear,
    We will look up to one stronger than we,
And if the Spring, sorrow doth bring,
    We will trust in our God, and to Him flee.

Through the Shadow.

I am sad and weary,
    All is dark within ;
All around is dreary,
    All around is sin.

And I'm sinking, sinking,
    Whither shall I turn ?
I am thinking, thinking,
    But my thoughts will burn.

Oh, my Blessed Savior,
    In this hour of need,
Shed on me Thy blessing,
    Shed Thy love on me.

Hark, I hear a whisper—
    But 'tis far away ;

Can'st Thou, Lord, draw nearer,
  Nearer unto me?

Yes, the voice grows nearer,
  And He smiles on me,
As my way grows clearer,
  And I my duty see.

Oh, ye wives and mothers,
  Though you're oft cast down,
If the Cross ye meekly bear,
  Ye shall wear the Crown.

Yes, the Crown of Glory—
  In that land above ,
In that land where Jesus lives,
  And where all is love.

My Guardian Angel

I feel a Holy Presence ever near,
Which keeps me from all thought of harm or fear,
Altho' no form or features do I see,
I feel the Presence near my heart to cheer.

Sometimes another form my fancies see,
The features, they look dark and grim to me,
'Tis then my Guardian Angel hastens near,
And that dark one draws back with look of fear.

For good and ill, they cannot dwell together,
But I can trust the loving Presence ever,
The Guardian Angel, sent by God divine,
To guard what He has given—this life of mine.

So there is never solitude for me,
For I am never quite alone you see,
And when my body unto death draws near,
I trust His Holy Presence ever dear.

A Sight Through the Window

Beautiful sights from my window I see,
Nowhere on earth can more beautiful be,
Wide spreading meadow with grass all so green,
And a large grove of trees in the distance are seen.

Then a gentle ascent to the top of a hill,

Where a bright wood is standing in majesty still,

With its leaves of all shades and variety seen,
And glistening there in the bright, glowing sun.

One tree all alone in its glory doth stand,
Just off to the left and the winds do it fan,
And it sways to and fro and rocks in the breeze,
And it looks just as if it was bowing to me.

Sway on, lovely tree, in your beauty so rare,
That is heightened so much by the sun's bright
    glare,
That dances and glances and thy radiance doth
    meet,
Like some bright, golden zephyr playing hide and
    seek.

The clouds are piled up in such beautiful shapes,
Just above the hill-tops their loveliness makes
Such an elegant picture through my window for me,
If I were an artist, it on canvas you'd see.

How many sweet pictures are lost to the view
Of the world, because of the incompetent few
Who can appreciate them, but do not know how
To show them to others on canvas, you know.

A Whisper

Sweet music comes to me of flowing water,
As it goes hurrying onward to the river,
'Tis but a little spring hastening hither,
Yet it sweet music brings unto me ever.

Why do you hurry so, sweet spring water?
Wait awhile, let us go water the meadow,
O do not be in haste, wait till to-morrow,
There is enough water now in the river.

You're such a little thing, sweet spring water,
You will be swallowed up in that big river,
Better come and stay with me, sweet little rover,
Do not be hurrying and working forever.

But a soft whisper comes, " Tempt me not, stranger,
I have my duties and must do them ever,
God alone knoweth best, why I go there,
Can I not trust myself to his kind care?"

So it goes onward, ne'er turning aside,
But to the laws of God, fast doth abide,
Bringing a blessing unto our poor hearts,
Bidding us not from our God to depart.

Lines on the Death of Longfellow

Father, there comes gently knocking
  At the heavenly portal, there,
One, who's shed o'er life the sunshine
  Of his spirit, bright and fair.
Let the angels hasten quickly,
  Open wide the heavenly door,
Who more fitted, Lord, to enter,
  Enter at the heavenly door?
Earth has lost, by death, a poet,
  One whose works will still remain,
Gladdening many a life of sorrow,
  Soothing many a life of pain ;
Raising many a brother's courage,
  Keeping them from sin and stain.
Who more worthy, Lord, to enter
  That bright, lovely, fair domain?
All through life, the flowers he's scattered,
  And they float from shore to shore,
Setting forth the blessed example
  Of a life so bright and pure,
Nobly has he done his life-work,
  And his fame will spread the more,
All down through the distant ages,
  Gladdening homes all the world o'er ;
Yet we know that to his heart,
  Has come sorrow, grief and care,
But Thou in Thy love hast kept him—
  Did not let his heart despair.

For otherwise, how could it be ?
  In a life like his so fine,
For grief and sorrow purify,
  And like gold the life will shine.
Some have talents, bright and clear,
  In others, they are more obscure,
But like a gardener, each must bear
  The heat of day, if they procure
The greatest good, each from their own
  Bringing forth the brightest flowers ;
And the seed that they have sown
  Will sometimes watered be—with tears.
Help us, Father, with Thy love,
  So to bear the burden here,
That when we are called above,
  We may something have to leave,
That the world may better be
  For our having in it lived,
And that we may daily feel
  That Thou dost approval give.

Be Thankful

Be thankful for thy talents,
  Tho' small they seem to be ;
For have they not been given,
  To be of use to thee ?

Perhaps thy blest example
  Set forth in these may.be

The means of leading some one
  Unto the Blessed Tree

Of life and light and love—
  Be shed within the soul
Of some poor wandering ones,
  Ere they have reached the shoal;

And are far beyond the help
  Of mortal hand to stay,
Their swift and onward feet
  Adown the dangerous way.

Then, Lord, will we be thankful,
  For the talents Thou hast given,
And feel that we can trust to Thee,
  To lead them on to Heaven.

A Contented Mind is a Continual Feast

We humbly bow to Thee,
  Great God above,
In all Thy works, we see
  Thy wondrous love.

The mighty **oak** doth stand
  So firm for Thee,
The little flowers proclaim
  Thy majesty.

Oh then why should not we,
  Thy children, be
Contented with our lot,
  Whate'er it be.

Only a Penny

Johnny had a penny
  Whirling it around,
There upon the table,
  'Twas one that he had found.
Little penny bright and new,
  Going 'round so fast,
Whirling round and shining so,
  Made little Johnny laugh.

Sometimes to the very edge
   The little penny came,
But Johnny would put out his hand
   And send it back again,
But somehow in whirling it
   A little bit too fast,
The penny came unto the edge
   And tumbled off at last.

And straightway to the cupboard
   The little penny ran,
And up jumps little Johnny
   To catch it if he can,
And so he runs and gets the broom
   And he goes poking 'round,
But as he brings it out again
   No penny can be found.

But there was a little hole
   Just in the corner there,
A little mouse had made it,
   It made poor Johnny stare,
But Johnny is a little man,
   He's not a going to cry,
But he, in setting up the broom,
   Saw sticking there so sly,
His little penny bright and new,
   He was glad he did not cry.

But Johnny he liked candy,
   So to the store he went,
The store it was so handy,

And soon his penny spent,
But when the candy made him sick
And he was suffering pain,
Then little Johnny wished he had
His penny back again.

And if he had it back
He'd put it up and save,
Perhaps he then some more could make
And soon a dollar have,
And then he'd buy a little farm
And on it he would live,
And with his horse and carriage,
To town he then would drive.

But be careful, boys, how you get
The money that you have,
And never cheat another,
But be honest, true and brave,
For stealing, lying, cheating—
It is a wicked sin,
And only direst trouble
Unto your life will bring.

Lamentation

MOTHER

My little one is gone, Oh, woe is me,
Why should the Lord so soon take him away?
The bitter tears I shed but make me worse;
Oh, why should upon me rest this deep curse?

FRIEND

Mother, thy flower has flown, yet do not weep,
It is not dead, but entered that deep sleep,
From which no earthly power can ever wake.
But God above, thy little child did take,
Its little feet to guide in paths above,
Where there is naught of sorrow, only love.
We may not know the reason why he takes,
So soon the little life which He has given,
And our hearts in their deep anguish nearly break;
It may be one more link 'twixt us and heaven,
To keep our hearts more firmly bound to Him,
Till we this earthly path, no more shall tread,
And we have left below, our load of sin,
Until our soul, unto its God has fled.

Ode to the Moon

Beautiful moon, thou art looking so bright,
Shedding thy gleams through the cold, still night,
Earthward thou art sending thy radiant rays,
Making the night resemble the day.

One little star, doth thee company keep,
Like a sweet child in thy smile so deep,
Shedding together thy smiles so clear—
Scattering the shadows so dark and drear.

Where are the other bright stars to-night?
Have they wandered off to some distant height?
Or are they covered by the wandering clouds,
Wholly enrapt in their misty shrouds?

Or are they thy children, sweet mother moon,
And hast thou put them to bed so soon,
Under the covers their bright eyes keep,
Until they drop into a sweet sound sleep?

That one little star must a favorite be,
As thou lettest it sit up alone with thee;
Or is it of all thy children fair,
The eldest, to so much privilege share?

Why canst thou not speak to us, silvery moon?
Thy loving smile dispels the gloom
Of our hearts, and we would know thee better,
By conversation, as well as by letter.

The astronomers tell us wonderful things of thee,

But how they can know, we do not see,
And then again their opinions differ,
And when they are done, we know thee no better.

Canst thou not send us that little star,
If it be a daughter of thine so fair,
That she may to us the mystery sing,
And tidings of thee to us may bring?

Or is she engaged to the King of Day,
That thou keepest thy watch so diligently,
And will the wedding take place on the heights
     over yonder,
Where day and night will be joined together?

That Old Steam Engine

Rattle, rattle, bang, bang,
Puff, puff, whang, whang,
'Tis that old steam engine
Making such confusion,
To which I make allusion.

For in a factory we do live,
Where in the summer, they make cheese ;
But now they are cider-making,
Bringing apples and cider taking,
The many teams all day are going,
Back and forth which makes confusion.

But the rooms so pleasant are,
That we do not mind the noise,

Only once in awhile, I fear,
It makes us cross to see the boys
Running and romping through the yard,
And swing so much on our clothes line.

Now their ways I can't approve,
Of giving cider unto boys,
Of course we know 'tis very good,
And in itself, no harm it does,
But it creates in them desires,
And something stronger they require.

The engine and boiler there you see,
It goes all right with just enough steam,
But if too much steam you do put on,
It bursts the boiler and does much harm,
So boys with drink and influence strong,
Bring others with themselves to wrong.

I am not like some to say,
The cider-barrel I can bless,
For when the cider getteth strong,
It's dangerous, I must confess,
And if such habits they do make,
'Twill be so hard for them to break.

A Summer Shower

How delicious is the greeting
  Of a summer shower to me,
When the heat is so oppressive,
  That one can hardly see.

And I love to watch the drops,
  As they spatter on the walk,
And they spatter up again,
  As if they were loth to stop.

And my little daughter,
  Little midget, she,
Hovers near the window,
  Chatting merrily.

Oh, they make such pleasant music,
  By taking the twain,
The sound of baby voices,
  And the patter of the rain.

Perplexities

One night, as I tried to settled be,
To write a few lines of poetry,
My baby cried and fretted for me,
And I could not get her to quiet be.

I rocked and sung and sung and rocked,
And after awhile, I stock still stopped ;

And then it was, oh, strange to say,
To the land of dreams, she wandered away.

Sweet baby—she looked so white,
And when she's awake, she is so bright,
And I thought—Oh, what if life should go
On beyond, and come back no more.

Then I said, "I will love you while I may,
Soon for ought I know, there may come a day
When through the gates, thou'lt wend thy way,
And do what I can—thou wilt not stay."

Foolish fancies, do you say?
They are only the thoughts of the mind, that stray
Back and forth, like the ocean spray,
And who can hinder them coming to me?

For they come unbidden, as I sit here,
And sometimes, in thinking, I drop a tear ;
For such sad thoughts will bring their sting,
And shadows o'er the mind will fling.

Twilight Meditation

It is at the edge of evening,
    In the quiet twilight hour,
When the sun has ceased its gleaming,
    And the earth is shaded o'er
With that soft and mellow light,
    And the work of day is done ;

But yet it is not night,
  Or the evening yet begun.
I am sitting with my children,
  Two sweet little girls are they,
And their eyes are growing heavy,
  They are tired out with play.
All day long they keep so busy,
  Running, laughing, full of song,
But just now they both are quiet,
  And to sleep will go ere long.
So I take them and undress them,
  And I put them both to bed,
Then the moon comes softly stealing
  In the room, and o'er us sheds
It's soft light so pale and still,
  Making all more quiet seem.
And my mind with thoughts so filled
  That I dread the lights to bring.
But the time is slowly passing,
  And we now must call it night ;
Husband soon will home be coming,
  And he loves to see the light
Through the windows brightly streaming,
  Shedding o'er his path its ray ;
For with business he'd be tired,
  Working, thinking, all the day.

What Maybell Said

Dropping on the window pane,
Comes the softly falling rain,
Making music, sweet and low,
And the vines sway to and fro,
With a soft and gentle breeze,
Which doth scarcely stir the trees.

Little children, sweet and fair,
Peeping thro' the window there,
Wondering at the drops so bright,
Shining in the bright sunlight,
Little angels in disguise,
Gazing with such wondering eyes.

Looking upward now they spy,
Stretching clear across the sky,
The rainbow with its colors bright,
Red and blue and pink and white,
And they both begin to cry,
" Mamma, see up in the sky."

Then I ask them what it is,
Shining up above the trees?
Blanchie says she doesn't know,
And to studying off she goes,

Maybell who can scarcely talk,
Thinks it is the Lord's side-walk.

Strange ideas such children have,
Which on their minds, impressions leave,
And in years to come will they,
In their minds live o'er this day,
When they from their window took,
At the rainbow, their first look.

A Nutting We Will Go

Bring the horse up to the door,
    Haste thee now and do not tarry,
And a-nutting we will go,
    All along the pleasant valley.

We will hie unto the wood,
    It is such a lovely day,
It will do the children good,
    Come now, let us haste away.

Bring the baskets and a sack,
    And put on a common dress,
So that we may nothing lack,
    To make our nutting a success.

And a luncheon, too, we'll bring,
    We can eat it in the shadow,
Of the wood, the crumbs we'll fling
    To the birdies there that warble.

And hickory nuts in such profusion,
With flowers and grass and mosses neat,
Ah, surely it is no delusion.

The frost has loosened up the burrs,
So they'd come off with just a shaking,
O, isn't it the height of fun,
To go on such a merry-making?

The children make the woodland ring,
With their light laugh and merry singing,
The sun shines out in roseate gleams,
As we oft see it ere its setting.

And so we think it time to start,
And so they bring the faithful horse,
With sack and baskets brimming full,
We soon again will be at home.

Light the lamp, dear mother, now,
  And we around it will make merry,
Merry as a summer's day,
  As we chase dull care away.

Dew Drops

Dew drops on the hillside,
  Dew drops in the air,
Dew drops in the meadow,
  Dew drops everywhere.
Dew drops on the house-tops,
  Dew drops in the grass,
So we get our feet wet,
  As we saunter past.

But, my little dew drops,
  You must now beware,
For slowly o'er the hill-tops,
  The sun is peeping there.
And when he climbs up over,
  With warmer, brighter rays,
Shining little dew drops,
  Must surely pass away.

So the Living Son,
  Our little children takes,
In His own bright home,
  They do us await ;

And when He in glory,
   In the East doth come,
We will see our dew drops
   Shining 'round His Throne.

Temptation

One day as I was looking from my window at the
    park,
For we lived just across the way—'twas in McHenry
    block,
I saw a young man, dressed in black, come reeling
    down the street,
And when he came into the park, he sat down in a
    seat,
His head kept nodding, nodding, and he straightway
    went to sleep.

And by and by an officer came strolling down the
    street,
Of course it was a wicked sin to see him sprawling so,
And so the officer thought that he must surely go,
And so he took him by the arm, and tried him to
    awake,
Of course the man was sleepy, and he needed quite a
    shake.

When he awoke, he did not think that this was hardly
    right,
So up he got, and soon began the officer to fight;

But the officer was strong of arm, and so with all his
 might,
He got him by the collar, but such a woeful fright.

He marched him 'round the corner and out of sight
 away,
Whatever did become of him, I'm sure I could not
 say,
And yet it is a common thing, to see a young man
 thus,
A wavering and staggering and falling in the dust,
But surely it is not the way that everything should be.

Come, let us take a little walk around a bit, and see,
Looking in the window there, what do you see, I
 pray?
Wine in shining bottles stare in such a tempting way ;
And if a man but have the taste, it's hard to pass it by,
It's dreadful for the drinking man, however hard he
 try.

With his eyes bulging out, I have seen the strong
 man stand,
Clutching little children, and a razor in his hand,
But the frenzy passed away, and the deed it was not
 done,
And the Bible then he took and in prayer, he knelt
 him down.

Be careful, O my brother, how you tempt another so,

How you cause a weeping family, such bitterness to
  know,
But turn thy back upon it, before it is too late,
And help a wandering brother, for thine own soul's
  sake.

The Little German

I knew a little German,
  He lived in our town,
From Germany he came,
  When he was rather young.

He was a fine shoe-maker,
  That's what they all did say,
He would finish up the shoes
  In such a nice, fine way.

But he got tired of making shoes,
  He must more money make,
And he must make it easier,
  So a saloon he'd take.

He never did intend to drink,
  He'd only sell, you know,
Let the other fellows drink,
  He would get the dollars so.

'Twas but a short time after that?
  We met him on the street,

His eyes they looked so bleary,
　　And his clothes not very neat.

And then a short time after that,
　　We heard that he was dead,
It was the drink that killed him,
　　That's what the neighbors said.

And so he sold the liquor
　　To give himself a boost,　·
But well we know his chickens
　　Did all come home to roost.

He was his own best customer,
　　'Tis often quite that way,
But oh, dear Lord, have pity,
　　Upon him in that day.

Memories

Out through the window from the lawn,
　　Comes the sound of pattering feet,
Dear little children, hurrying on,
　　With merry laughter my ears they greet.

All in their innocence and truth,
　　Heedless of the morrow's care,
All in their beauty, health and youth,
　　Dear Lord, bless them, is my prayer.

Out on the hill-side, not far away,
　　On this cold and wintry day,

Dear little heads are laid so low,
    Buried so deeply under the snow.
One by one we laid them there,
    Free from sorrow, care and pain,
Well we know that those He takes,
    Never can come back again.

Up above the azure blue,
    Up in heaven, clear and bright,
Little spirits that we knew,
    'Round God's Throne, all clothed in white.

Singing songs so sweet and new,
    Glorious anthems, heavenly strains,
God has blessed them, that we know,
    Of His ways we can't complain.

God in wisdom took away,
    Half my children from the nest,
Half remain with me to-day,
    Surely we would call Him blest.

But a few short years have flown,
    It but seems as yesterday,
They to man's estate have grown,
    Strong, true hearts to lead the way.

FINIS